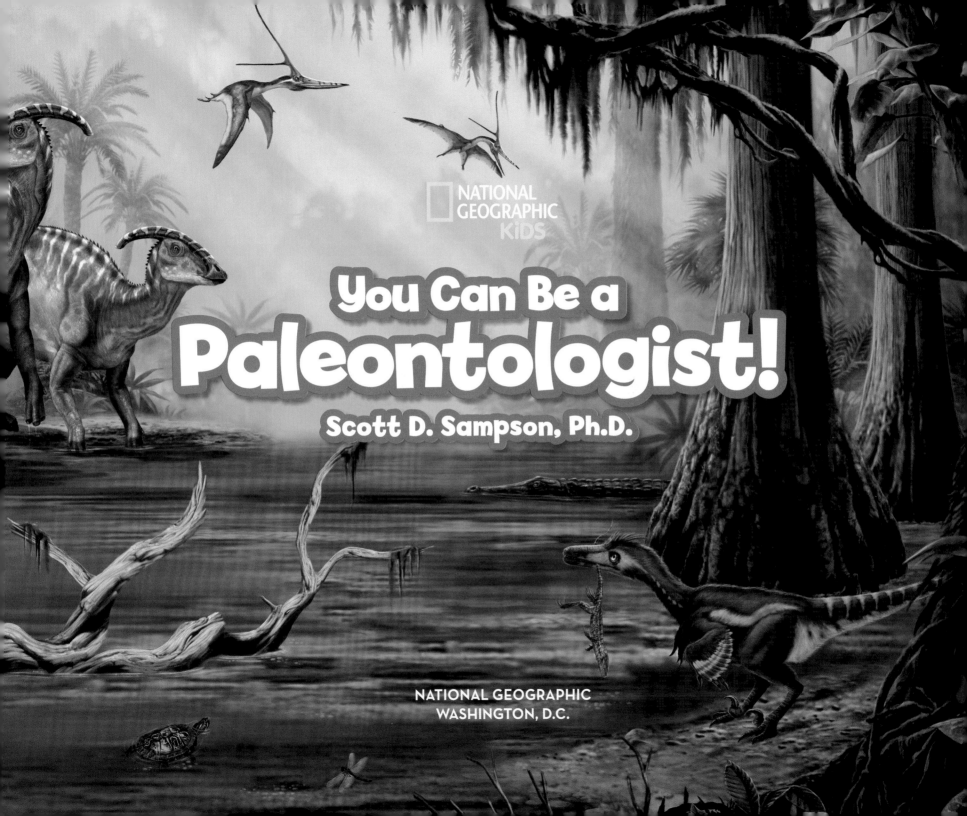

You Can Be a
Paleontologist!

Scott D. Sampson, Ph.D.

NATIONAL GEOGRAPHIC
WASHINGTON, D.C.

What is paleontology?

Hi! My name is Dr. Scott, and I'm a paleontologist.

DR. SCOTT AND HIS TEAM WORK TO DIG UP FOSSILS.

A paleontologist is a scientist who studies fossils—the remains of plants and animals that lived a long, long time ago.

Some paleontologists search for ancient mammals. Others find fossils of plants, seashells, or fish. Some of these prehistoric plants and animals lived millions of years before that amazing group of reptiles known as dinosaurs.

Me, I love dinosaurs. I loved dinosaurs as a kid, and I still love them today. Some people say I never grew up! I love to find dinosaur fossils and think about what these animals and their world looked like millions of years ago.

Let's learn about the kinds of things paleontologists do! We'll start out hunting for dinosaur fossils. Then we'll dig them up, get them to a museum, glue the fossils back together, and study them in search of clues about prehistoric worlds.

At the end, I'll tell you a BIG secret . . .

Are you ready? Let's go!

PLANT FOSSIL

SEASHELL FOSSIL

MAMMAL FOSSIL

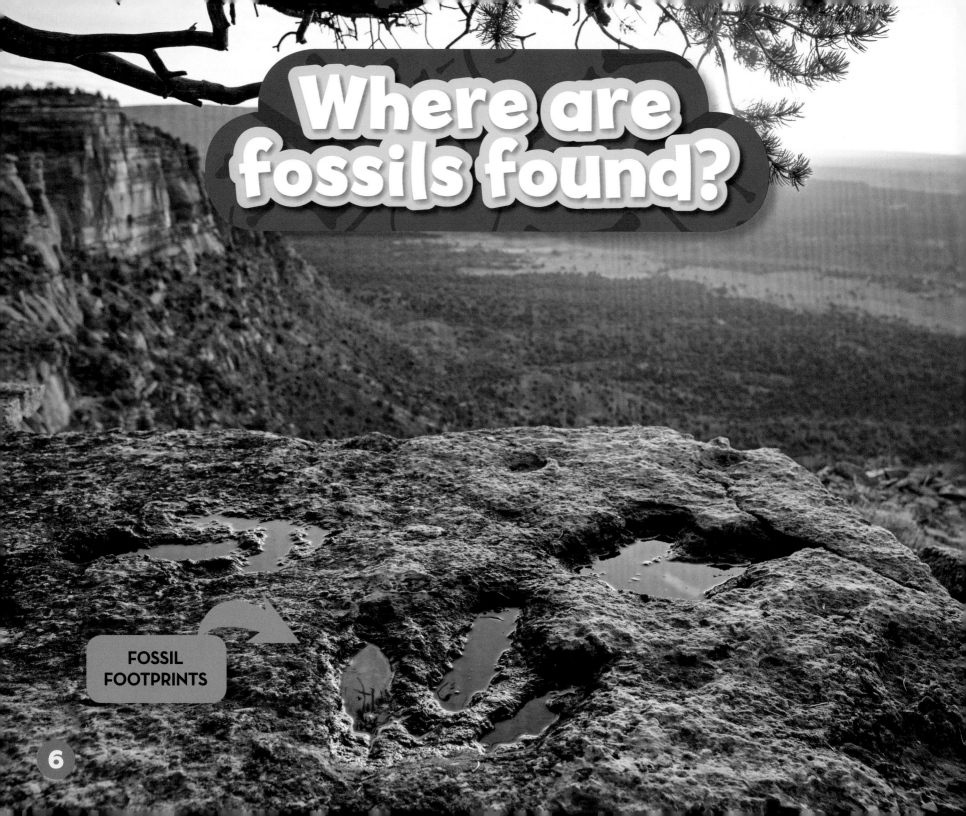

Where are fossils found?

FOSSIL
FOOTPRINTS

The first step is to get out there and find some fossils! Believe it or not, dinosaur bones have been found on every continent. So if we want to discover dinosaurs, there are plenty of places to look.

Many fossils are found in "badlands," like Grand Staircase-Escalante National Monument in southern Utah, U.S.A. I've worked there for many years.

These places are called badlands because they're so dry and rugged. It's hard to grow food or raise animals there.

But for paleontologists, these are the good lands! Fossils are buried in rocks, so it's much easier to find fossils in places without a lot of plants covering the ground.

Because badlands are so hilly, they usually don't have many roads. So if we want to discover dinosaurs here, we'll have to do a lot of walking!

FOSSILS HAVE EVEN BEEN FOUND IN ANTARCTICA!

PALEONTOLOGISTS HIKE THROUGH THE BADLANDS IN UTAH.

7

How do you find fossils?

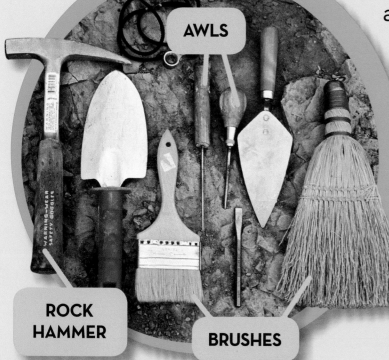

BACKPACK WITH TOOLS

AWLS

ROCK HAMMER

BRUSHES

If we want to go out finding fossils, the first thing to do is get a backpack with the right gear. We'll need fossil-digging tools, like brushes, awls, glue, and a rock hammer. Be sure to bring along pencils, pens, a notebook, and a camera. Oh, and don't forget your lunch, sunscreen, and plenty of drinking water!

Next, we'll head to a place where people have found dinosaur bones or other fossils before. It's always best to start where we know fossils can be found.

If we find something that looks like a piece of fossil but we're not sure, we can try touching it to our tongues. Fossils have tiny pores that make them stick to your tongue. Rocks don't!

Over time, fossils at Earth's surface tend to break into small fragments. Then they get washed down the hill when it rains. So once we've found some bits of fossil, follow the fragments up the hill. We'll keep going until we can't see any more of them.

Finally, we'll dig into the rock and try to find where the fossil fragments came from. If we're very lucky, we'll find more fossils. We may even discover the skull or skeleton of a new species that no one has ever seen before!

YOU CAN TELL ROCKS FROM FOSSILS WITH YOUR TONGUE! BUT ALWAYS ASK AN ADULT BEFORE PUTTING ANYTHING FROM THE GROUND INTO YOUR MOUTH.

USING AN AWL AND A BRUSH TO UNCOVER A FOSSIL

How do paleontologists dig up fossils?

Now that we've found part of a dinosaur, or some other prehistoric creature, it's time to dig it up!

The first step in an excavation is to remove the rock layers above the bones. That means digging with tools like big picks and shovels, sometimes working in the hot sun for many days, or even weeks. If the rock is extra hard, we may need large power tools like jackhammers or rock saws.

Once enough rock is removed, we'll get down close to the fossils. Now it's time to switch back to smaller hand tools. We'll need rock hammers, awls, and brushes to carefully excavate the rock covering the bones.

Most fossil bones have cracks going through them. So as the rock is removed and the fossil is exposed, we put a thin coating of glue on the bone. That will hold the pieces together.

Be sure to uncover only a small part of the fossil. We'll want to leave most of it encased in rock for protection. Oh, and we'll need to remember to take photographs and carefully draw a map so that we know exactly where each bone was found!

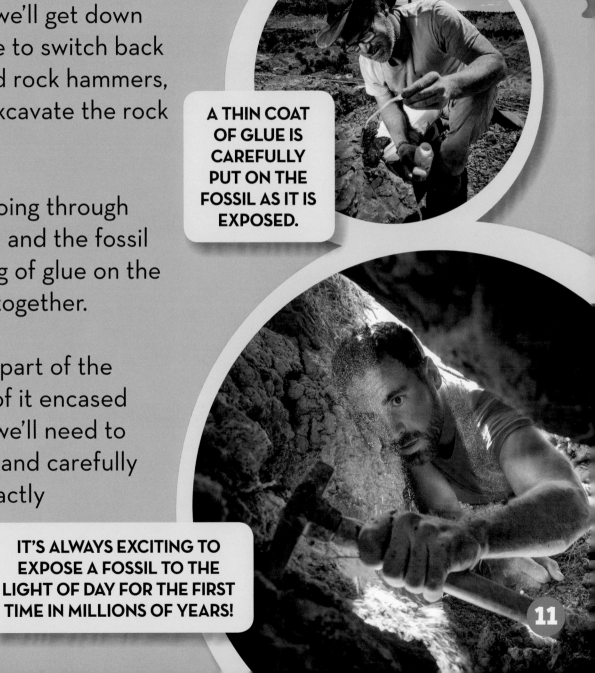

A THIN COAT OF GLUE IS CAREFULLY PUT ON THE FOSSIL AS IT IS EXPOSED.

IT'S ALWAYS EXCITING TO EXPOSE A FOSSIL TO THE LIGHT OF DAY FOR THE FIRST TIME IN MILLIONS OF YEARS!

How are fossils removed from the field?

SOMETIMES PALEONTOLOGISTS HAVE TO GET CREATIVE WHEN REMOVING LARGE FOSSILS!

For more than a hundred years, paleontologists have been using a special three-step technique called plaster jackets to protect fossils.

Step 1 is to mix up a bucket of plaster and water.

Step 2 is to dip strips of a rough fabric called burlap into the wet plaster.

Step 3 is to cover the fossil with these plaster-coated strips.

After the plaster dries, the fossil can be flipped over so that more layers of plaster and burlap can be applied. Once the fossil is safely encased in its plaster jacket, it's ready to be moved!

If the fossil is small, we can carry it out in a backpack. Somewhat bigger fossils can be tied down to a stretcher and carried out by several people. Scientists need to get creative in the field! You never know what you'll need to do to move a fossil.

FOSSILS BEING WRAPPED IN BURLAP AND PLASTER

IF THE FOSSIL IS REALLY BIG, IT WILL NEED TO BE FLOWN OUT BY HELICOPTER!

13

How are fossils prepared in the lab?

A FOSSIL IN THE PREPARATION LAB

When I find a fossil, I bring it back to the museum. Some fossils go into a storage room to await preparation. But if it's a really important find, like a new kind of dinosaur, it goes straight to the preparation lab!

The preparators—the people who work in the lab—first remove the plaster jacket from one side of the fossil using a small power saw.

The next step is to begin taking away more rock so that the newly exposed pieces of the fossil can be glued back together. For this part, the preparator uses a variety of tools.

Power tools help to grind away big chunks of rock. Smaller tools, like dental picks (yes, the same kind your dentist uses), are great for carefully removing the rock that is touching the fossil.

This is hard work that requires a lot of patience. A fossil preparator may take more than a year to clean and glue back together a single fossil!

REMOVING THE PLASTER JACKET

PIECING TOGETHER A FOSSIL

Where are fossils stored?

FOSSIL COLLECTIONS ARE STORED IN A HUGE ROOM INSIDE THE MUSEUM KNOWN AS THE COLLECTION AREA.

Imagine a huge room brimming with thousands of fossils. This is the museum's collection area. Most of these fossils will never make it out into the museum's exhibition halls. There are simply too many of them!

Every fossil has its own special number. And a label nearby lists things like the name of the animal, where and when it was discovered, and the name of the person who found it.

But these fossils don't just sit around collecting dust.

Believe it or not, this room is where paleontologists go to make discoveries! Sometimes they make these discoveries many years after the fossils are prepared and put away for storage.

BECAUSE FOSSIL COLLECTIONS ARE SO BIG, ONLY A SMALL NUMBER OF FOSSILS ARE EVER DISPLAYED IN MUSEUMS.

How do paleontologists study fossils?

Paleontologists are like detectives, seeking clues to solve ancient mysteries. The first step is to ask questions. For example:

What did the animal eat?
How did the animal move?

To answer questions like these, we use many tools to look for clues. A microscope can be used to see tiny bumps on teeth. These can tell us a lot about what the animal ate. A CT scanner might peer into a skull, revealing secrets about the size of the dinosaur's brain or its sense of smell.

A CT SCANNER CAN BE USED TO LOOK INSIDE A FOSSIL WITHOUT HAVING TO BREAK INTO IT.

Other clues can help us figure out what species of dinosaur we've found. For example, if our fossil is from a horned dinosaur—like my favorite, *Kosmoceratops*—we might compare its bones with those of other horned dinosaurs. That way we could figure out if the fossils were from a known species or from some creature never seen before.

Or maybe we want to know if our dinosaur could run fast. Then we might compare the leg bones of our new discovery with those of fast-running animals like horses or cheetahs.

The important thing is to keep asking questions and seeking clues. Then we can come up with possible answers, or hypotheses, to help us solve the mystery.

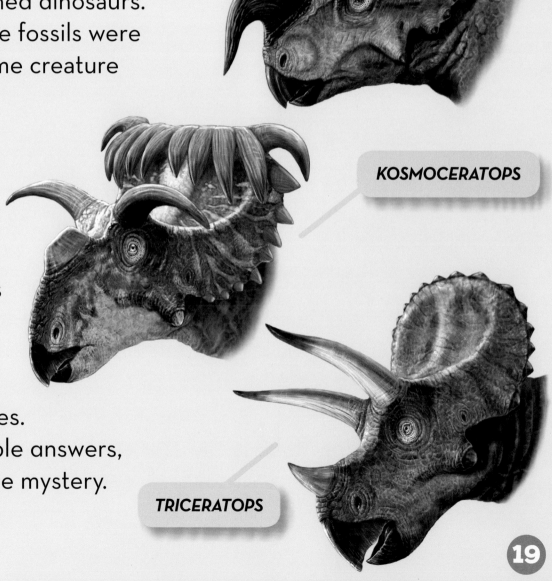

EINIOSAURUS

KOSMOCERATOPS

TRICERATOPS

19

Why did some dinosaurs look so strange?

Another great reason to study fossils is to figure out why dinosaurs look so strange! Some dinosaurs had horns and crests. Others had plates and spikes. Still others had bony clubs on their tails. How did dinosaurs use all these crazy features?

To find answers, paleontologists often look at the strange features of animals living today, like the antlers of deer and the horns of antelope.

Some weird-looking features of dinosaurs—like the tail spikes of *Stegosaurus*—may have been used to fight off predators. Other strange features—like the horns on the back of the *Kosmoceratops* skull—were likely used for showing off.

A *STEGOSAURUS* USES ITS TAIL
TO BATTLE AN *ALLOSAURUS*.

21

What did dinosaurs eat?

For most kinds of dinosaurs, we don't know the exact foods they preferred. But, by studying the teeth and jaws of dinosaurs and making comparisons with animals living today, paleontologists can learn a lot.

Dinosaur carnivores, like *Tyrannosaurus*, tend to have sharp, pointy teeth with tiny serrations, just like on a steak knife. These teeth were used for stabbing and tearing apart meat. That's just like the living great white shark!

GREAT WHITE SHARK

TYRANNOSAURUS (CARNIVORE)

The teeth of dinosaur herbivores, like *Triceratops*, aren't as pointy as those of carnivores. The teeth of herbivores also tend to be packed closely together, just like we see in deer and other living plant-eaters.

We think that some dinosaurs, like the toothless *Ornithomimus*, were omnivores. That is, they ate both plants and meat. *Ornithomimus* and its close relatives were fast runners, and their toothless beaks would have been good for grabbing small animals, as well as for eating plants.

TRICERATOPS (HERBIVORE)

DEER

ORNITHOMIMUS (OMNIVORE)

CASSOWARY

23

What was the Earth like when dinosaurs lived?

PLANT FOSSILS

When paleontologists head out to the badlands, we search for a lot more than just dinosaur bones. We want to know what the place was like when dinosaurs lived there. We want to know things like:

Was it wet or dry?
What other kinds of animals and plants were there?

So we search for lots more clues.

Today, the badlands in southern Utah—where *Kosmoceratops* lived—are part of a hot, dry desert. But we've found plenty of fossils of water-loving animals there, like fish, turtles, and crocodiles. They lived millions of years ago, at the same time as *Kosmoceratops*.

FOSSILS AND OTHER CLUES TELL US THAT THE LAND WAS WARM AND SWAMPY WHEN *KOSMOCERATOPS* ROAMED UTAH MILLIONS OF YEARS AGO DURING THE CRETACEOUS TIME PERIOD.

Are dinosaurs still alive today?

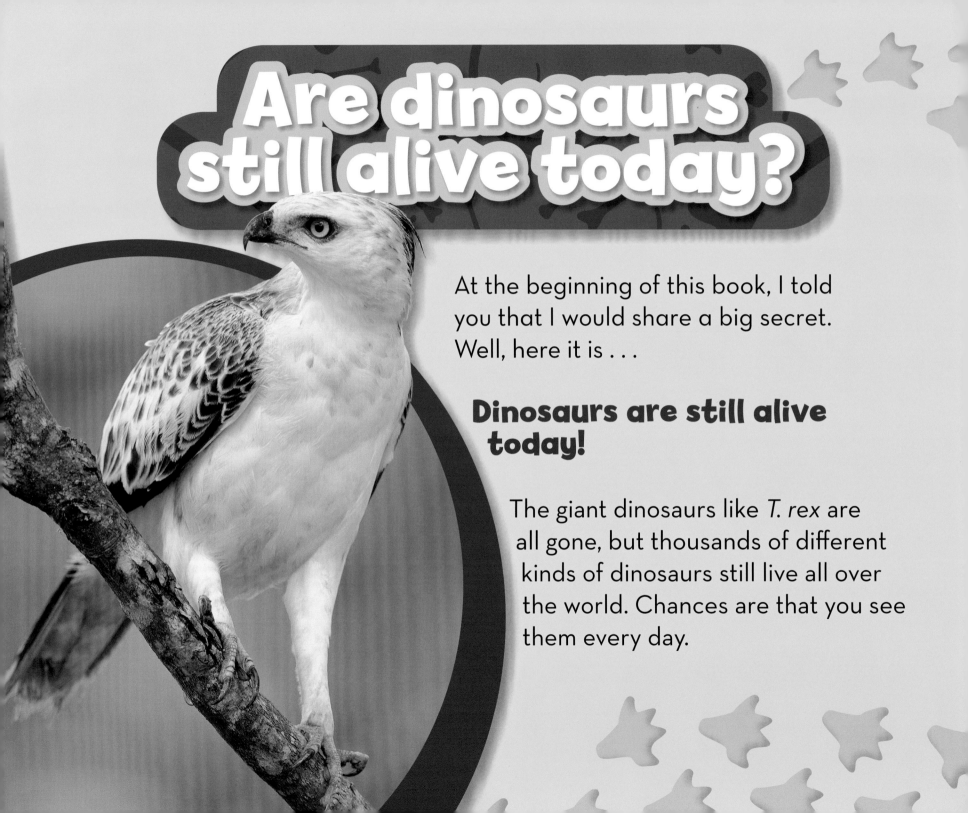

At the beginning of this book, I told you that I would share a big secret. Well, here it is . . .

Dinosaurs are still alive today!

The giant dinosaurs like *T. rex* are all gone, but thousands of different kinds of dinosaurs still live all over the world. Chances are that you see them every day.

We call them birds!

All birds are closely related to small, meat-eating dinosaurs like *Velociraptor* that lived way back in the Mesozoic era, the "Age of Dinosaurs." Many features of birds, like feathers, appeared first in raptor dinosaurs like these.

We know this because paleontologists have discovered lots of dinosaurs with feathers. Some even had wings! *Microraptor*, for example, was a four-winged dinosaur (and not a bird) that probably climbed trees and used its wings to glide to the ground.

So eagles, owls, robins, and hummingbirds are not only birds. They're dinosaurs too! And if you like to eat chicken and turkey, guess what? You like to eat dinosaurs!

MICRORAPTOR

VELOCIRAPTOR

27

How do I become a paleontologist?

We've learned all about discovering, digging up, preparing, and studying fossils. But there are a few more things to keep in mind if you want to be a paleontologist. Here are some hints to help you along your path.

1 Learn as much as you can about all kinds of science. If you're going to study fossils, you'll need to know a lot about animals and plants living today, as well as those that lived a long time ago. You'll also need to understand how rocks formed and how Earth and life have changed over time.

2 Spend a lot of time out in nature. It's great to visit faraway places like national parks, but you can probably find plenty of nature close to where you live. You can even go looking for those dinosaurs known as birds! Most paleontologists I know spent lots of time playing in nature when they were kids.

3 Work on your fossil-finding skills by discovering things like rocks, insects, plants, bird feathers, and even fossils! You can make a "nature table" for your collection, kind of a mini-museum that will help you learn how to study all kinds of nature, including fossils.

MOST OF ALL, REMEMBER:
GET OUTSIDE,
GET INTO NATURE, AND MAKE
YOUR OWN DISCOVERIES!

GLOSSARY

Awl. A small, pointed hand tool used by paleontologists for removing rock from around fossils

Badlands. Hilly places with few plants, lots of exposed rocks, and sometimes many fossils

Burlap. A heavy fabric that can be cut into strips, dipped in plaster, and wrapped around fossils in the field so that they can be safely transported

Carnivore. An animal that eats only meat

CT scanner. A machine used by paleontologists to look inside fossils, especially skulls, without having to break into them

Excavation. A fossil dig site

Fossil. The remains of an ancient plant, animal, or other life-form that have been at least partially replaced by rock

Herbivore. An animal that eats only plants

Hypothesis. An idea you can test

Jackhammer. A large power tool used by paleontologists to break up rock around fossils

Microscope. A tool used by paleontologists to look at tiny features on fossils

Museum collection area. The place where fossils (and other kinds of objects) are stored and cared for

Omnivore. An animal that eats plants and meat

Paleontologist. A scientist who studies fossils

Plaster jacket. A coating of plaster and burlap used to protect fossils so that they can be safely transported

Preparation lab. The place where fossils are prepared, including removal of rock and gluing of broken fossil pieces

Preparator. The person who cleans fossils in the preparation lab

Rock hammer. A special hammer carried by paleontologists and geologists (scientists who study rocks), used for breaking into the rock

Rock saw. A power tool with a diamond-studded blade used by paleontologists to cut through rock around fossils

Serrations. Tiny bumps lining the teeth of meat-eating dinosaurs, used for tearing flesh

CREDITS

Many thanks to my mother, Catherine June Sampson, for igniting my lifelong passion for dinosaurs. Thanks also to my wife, Toni, and my daughters, Jade and Twangemeka, for their stalwart support. I am grateful to Mrs. Smith, my kindergarten teacher at Southlands Elementary School, for using dinosaurs to attract the attention of a distracted child. Warm thanks also to the paleontology staff and volunteers at the Denver Museum of Nature & Science, and to the many paleontology researchers and volunteers who have worked in Grand Staircase-Escalante National Monument. I dedicate this book to the millions of children around the world for whom, generation after generation, dinosaurs are an inspiring first foray into science.

The author and publisher also wish to sincerely thank the book team:

Shelby Alinsky, Kathryn Robbins, Jeff Heimsath, Joan Gossett, Kathryn Williams, and Anne LeongSon.

Title page: The skull of *Kosmoceratops*, a many-horned dinosaur discovered in Utah

Text copyright © 2017 Scott D. Sampson

Compilation copyright © 2017 National Geographic Partners, LLC

All rights reserved. Reproduction of the whole or any part of the contents without written permission from the publisher is prohibited.

NATIONAL GEOGRAPHIC and Yellow Border Design are trademarks of the National Geographic Society, used under license.

Since 1888, the National Geographic Society has funded more than 14,000 research, conservation, education, and storytelling projects around the world. National Geographic Partners distributes a portion of the funds it receives from your purchase to National Geographic Society to support programs including the conservation of animals and their habitats. To learn more, visit natgeo.com/info.

For more information, visit nationalgeographic.com, call 1-877-873-6846, or write to the following address:

National Geographic Partners, LLC
1145 17th Street N.W.
Washington, DC 20036-4688 U.S.A.

For librarians and teachers: nationalgeographic.com/books/librarians-and-educators

More for kids from National Geographic: natgeokids.com

For rights or permissions inquiries, please contact National Geographic Books Subsidiary Rights: bookrights@natgeo.com

Designed by Kathryn Robbins
Illustrations by Franco Tempesta

Trade hardcover ISBN: 978-1-4263-2728-5
Reinforced library binding ISBN: 978-1-4263-2729-2

Printed in Canada
22/FC/5

Photo Credits:
Cover (CTR), Franco Tempesta; Cover (LO RT), Stuart Ruckman/Natural History Museum of Utah; Back Cover (LE), Cory Richards/National Geographic Image Collection; Back Cover (RT), Courtesy of Scott Sampson; Front Jacket Flap, Franco Tempesta; Back Jacket Flap, Courtesy of Scott Sampson; 1 (CTR), Cory Richards/National Geographic Image Collection; 2-3, Franco Tempesta; 4 (UP), Cory Richards/National Geographic Image Collection; 4 (LO), Courtesy of Scott Sampson; 5 (UP), Ira Block/National Geographic Image Collection; 5 (CTR), Kevin Schafer/Getty Images; 5 (LO), Roberto Machado Noa/Getty Images; 6 (CTR), Cory Richards/National Geographic Image Collection; 7 (UP), Dawn Nichols/iStockphoto/Getty Images; 7 (LO), Richard M. Wicker/Denver Museum of Nature & Science; 8 (UP), Cory Richards/National Geographic Image Collection; 8 (LO), Photo Researchers/Getty Images; 9 (UP), Courtesy of Brad Purdy/Bureau of Land Management-Montana/Dakotas; 9 (LO), Cory Richards/National Geographic Image Collection; 10-11, Cory Richards/National Geographic Image Collection; 12 (CTR), Louie Psihoyos/Corbis; 13 (UP), Lynn Johnson/National Geographic Image Collection; 13 (CTR), Scott Linnett/SDU-T/ZUMA Press; 13 (LO), Jon Austria/The Daily Times/AP Images; 14, Gabriel Bouys/AFP/Getty Images; 15 (UP), Richard M. Wicker/Denver Museum of Nature & Science; 15 (LO), Cory Richards/National Geographic Image Collection; 16, Cory Richards/National Geographic Image Collection; 17 (UP), Richard M. Wicker/Denver Museum of Nature & Science; 17 (LO), Cory Richards/National Geographic Image Collection; 18, Field Museum Library/Getty Images; 19, Franco Tempesta; 20, Cory Richards/National Geographic Image Collection; 21, Franco Tempesta; 22 (LE), Stephen Frink/Getty Images; 22 (RT), Franco Tempesta; 23 (UP RT), Franco Tempesta; 23 (LO RT), Franco Tempesta; 23 (CTR RT), Kevin M. McCarthy/Shutterstock; 23 (LO LE), Kevin Schafer/Minden Pictures; 24 (UP), Buddy Mayes/Getty Images; 24 (LO), Ira Block/National Geographic Image Collection; 25, Franco Tempesta; 26, Peter Waechtershaeuser/BIA/Minden Pictures; 27, Franco Tempesta; 28, Hero Images/Getty Images; 29 (UP), Paul Simcock/Getty Images; 29 (CTR), Nilky/iStockphoto/Getty Images; 29 (LO), gopause/Shutterstock; 31, Franco Tempesta; 32, Courtesy of Scott Sampson